ENGLAND
the people

Erinn Banting

A Bobbie Kalman Book

The Lands, Peoples, and Cultures Series

Crabtree Publishing Company

www.crabtreebooks.com

The Lands, Peoples, and Cultures Series

Created by Bobbie Kalman

Author
Erinn Banting
Editor
Sarah Cairns
Editorial director
Kathy Middleton
Photo research
Katherine Berti, Crystal Sikkens
Print coordinator and
  Prepress technician
Katherine Berti

First edition:
  Coordinating editor
  Ellen Rodger
  Project editor
  Sean Charlebois
  Production coordinator
  Rosie Gowsell
  Project development, design, editing, and photo research
  First Folio Resource Group, Inc.: Erinn Banting, Quinn Banting, Molly Bennett, Tom Dart, Greg Duhaney, Jaimie Nathan, Debbie Smith, Meighan Sutherland, Anikó Szocs
  Editing
  Carolyn Black
  Consultants
  Jane Higginbottom, Alex Lloyd, Chris Stephenson

Photographs
Alamy: Art Directors & TRIP: page 22 (bottom); World Religions Photo Library: page 23 (top)
Dreamstime: Gofer: cover; Lagron49: page 15 (top right); Raylip65: page 25 (top); Deniskelly: page 26 (bottom)
iStockphoto: pages 18–19, 28; kkgas: page 1; MivPiv: page 16 (top right); fotoVoyager: page 21 (bottom)
Library of Congress: page 11

London 2012: page 27 (bottom)
Photos.com/Getty Images: pages 12, 14 (left)
Shutterstock: pages 3, 6 (top), 7, 19 (top), 20 (bottom), 21 (top), 22 (top), 27 (top), 30; Ints Vikmanis: page 4; Kamira: pages 5 (top), 17 (bottom), 29; David Burrows: page 5 (bottom); dutourdumonde: page 15 (bottom); Baloncici: page 17 (top); Featureflash: page 24 (top); Padmayogini: page 24 (bottom); Sportsphotographer.eu: page 26 (top)
Thinkstock: pages 9, 16 (bottom left), 31
Wikimedia Commons: Rotatebot: page 6 (bottom); Albert Kretschmer: page 8; James William Edmund Doyle: pages 9 (top), 10 (bottom); www.azerbaijanrugs.com/mp/ eworth1.htm: page 10 (top); Jacques Louis David: page 13 (top); Nathaniel Currier: page 13 (bottom); Library of Congress: page 14 (right); U.S. National Archives and Records Administration: page 15 (top left); NotFromUtrecht: page 20 (top); Mvkulkarni23: page 25 (bottom)

Illustrations
Dianne Eastman: icon
David Wysotski, Allure Illustrations: back cover

Front cover: Newly married Prince William and Princess Catherine wave to fans as they leave Westminster Abbey after their wedding ceremony.

Title page: A group of women celebrate the royal wedding by painting the Union Jack flag on their faces and waving royal wedding flags.

Icon: Teapots and teacups, which appear at the head of each section, are used to serve England's most popular drink. Traders first brought tea to England from China in the 1600s.

Back cover: Red foxes live in wooded areas across England. These animals live alone unless they are raising their young.

Library and Archives Canada Cataloguing in Publication

Banting, Erinn, 1976-
    England : the people / Erinn Banting. -- Rev ed.

(The lands, peoples, and cultures series)
Includes index.
Issued also in electronic formats.
ISBN 978-0-7787-9830-9 (bound).--ISBN 978-0-7787-9833-0 (pbk.)

    1. England--Social conditions--Juvenile literature. I. Title.
II. Series: Lands, peoples, and cultures series

HN398.E5B35 2012   j942   C2012-902293-4

Library of Congress Cataloging-in-Publication Data

Banting, Erinn.
  England. The people / Erinn Banting. -- Rev. ed.
    p. cm. -- (The lands, peoples, and cultures series)
  "A Bobbie Kalman Book."
  Includes index.
  ISBN 978-0-7787-9830-9 (reinforced library binding : alk. paper) -- ISBN 978-0-7787-9833-0 (pbk. : alk. paper) -- ISBN 978-1-4271-7892-3 (electronic pdf) -- ISBN 978-1-4271-8007-0 (electronic html)
  1. England--Social life and customs--Juvenile literature. I. Title.

DA110.B28 2012
942--dc23
                                                    2012013778

Crabtree Publishing Company

www.crabtreebooks.com   1-800-387-7650

Printed in the U.S.A./052012/FA20120413

Published in Canada
Crabtree Publishing
616 Welland Ave.
St. Catharines, Ontario
L2M 5V6

Published in the United States
Crabtree Publishing
PMB 59051
350 Fifth Avenue, 59th Floor
New York, New York 10118

Published in the United Kingdom
Crabtree Publishing
Maritime House
Basin Road North, Hove
BN41 1WR

Published in Australia
Crabtree Publishing
3 Charles Street
Coburg North
VIC 3058

Contents

A royal tradition

Life in England

The English discuss politics, as well as other topics such as sports and music, at pubs. Pubs, the short form of "public houses," are places where people gather for a drink and a traditional meal such as fish and chips. The English also enjoy playing soccer, hiking, biking, and driving through the rolling hills of the countryside. Scattered across this beautiful landscape are clues to the island's rich past, including the ruins of walls and forts built by the ancient Romans and majestic castles that were once home to England's royal families.

England's national anthem, "God Save the Queen," plays at sporting events, on the radio, and in classrooms each morning. The song indicates how important the **monarchy** is to the history of England. Powerful kings and queens **conquered** many lands around the world and built England into a mighty **empire**.

England is on the island of Great Britain, in the North Atlantic Ocean. Scotland, to the north, and Wales, to the west, are also on the island. England is part of a country called the United Kingdom of Great Britain and Northern Ireland.

Changing times

England no longer controls the territories it once did in North America, Africa, Asia, and Australia. In some of its former colonies, the monarchy has a symbolic role. In England, some people think the monarchy is not needed at all.

People line the street to get a glimpse of Queen Elizabeth and Prince Philip as they leave a ceremony honoring the Queen's birthday.

People crowd Trafalgar Square in London, the capital city of England. The square was built to honor the people who died in the Battle of Trafalgar, fought between England and France in 1805.

Shoppers mill through Petticoat Lane, a market district in London.

Early mysteries

The Rollright Stones is a stone circle in southern England which, according to legend, is all that remains of a king and his army who were frozen by an evil witch.

Hundreds of thousands of years ago, a strip of land, called a land bridge, connected England with the rest of Europe. Early hunters crossed the bridge to England, following animal herds. The 500,000-year-old remains of one of these hunters, called Boxgrove Man, are the oldest in England. Boxgrove Man is named after the gravel pit in the south where **archaeologists** found part of his shin bone and two of his teeth.

Homes for the dead

Ancient peoples in England built barrows, or large stone tombs covered with earth, to bury their dead. Jewelry, arrowheads, tools, and pots were also placed in the barrows. West Kennet Long Barrow, in the south, is the largest barrow in England. Built in 3500 B.C., it looks like a giant hill with large boulders lined up at one end. The boulders block long, dark passages that lead to an underground chamber.

When archaeologists excavated, or dug up, the West Kennet Long Barrow in the 1950s, they discovered the remains of nearly 50 bodies in its underground chamber.

Stonehenge

England's early inhabitants also built large circles out of massive stones. Stonehenge, in southern England, is the best-known stone circle. Construction began around 3000 B.C. and took more than 2,000 years to complete. When Stonehenge was finished, it consisted of a large stone **altar** surrounded by a horseshoe-shaped wall of stones. Two circular walls made of stones that weighed as much as 44 tons (40 tonnes) each surrounded this structure. Today, only the altar stone, a large stone nearby called the heel stone, and several stones from the walls remain.

Explaining Stonehenge

The altar stone suggests that Stonehenge was used for religious ceremonies, but the stones may also have helped ancient people predict the movement of the sun, the moon, and other stars and planets. On June 21, the first day of summer, called Midsummer's Day in England, the sun's rays line up with the heel and altar stones.

Even more mysterious than why Stonehenge was built is how it was built. Hundreds of heavy stones, some of which were transported from as far away as Wales, could not have been carried by humans, especially before the wheel was invented. Historians speculate that the stones were either floated down rivers on rafts and then dragged to the spot, or rolled on logs across the countryside by slaves.

The town of Avebury stands amid the remains of a stone circle that was partially destroyed in the 1600s to make room for the town's expansion. Today, the circle is protected by law.

More circles

Along with Stonehenge, the remains of more than a hundred mysterious stone circles still stand in England. The Avebury stone circle, in southern England, was built in 3000 B.C. at the center of a village. People in the **Middle Ages** destroyed and buried the original circle because they feared it was used in **pagan** ceremonies. The circle was rebuilt in the 1900s and is now protected by the National Trust, an organization that helps preserve the English countryside, coastline, and gardens and buildings of historical importance.

Some people believe that Stonehenge was a palace that belonged to a magical race of kings and queens who could see the future and cure the sick.

 # Ages of invasion

A group of people from central Europe, called the Celts, invaded southern England in 700 B.C. They forced the Iberians, who came to England around 5000 B.C. from Spain, and the Beaker people, who came from present-day France around 2000 B.C., to the northern and western edges of the island. On their newly conquered land in the south, the Celts built hill forts surrounded by ramparts, or walls.

The Roman Empire

Armies of **Roman** soldiers arrived on England's shores in 55 B.C. and began to take over most of the Celts' land. Many Celts fled to Scotland, Wales, the southern tip of England, and Ireland. To protect themselves from the attacks of Celts trying to recapture their land, the Romans built Hadrian's Wall, which stretched for 73 miles (118 kilometers) along what is now England's northwestern border. Along the wall they built forts to keep out invaders.

Many Roman settlements developed into England's modern cities, such as London, in the southeast, and York, in the northeast. The Romans built beautiful churches in these settlements, where they taught the people of England about their religion, Roman Catholicism, which is a **denomination** of Christianity.

Invaders from north and south

The Romans' occupation of England ended in 410 A.D. because their empire could no longer afford to maintain its many territories. Another wave of invaders soon came from Scandinavia, a region in northern Europe, and from Germany. These were the Angles, Saxons, and Jutes. Peoples called the Frisians and Franks also arrived from France, Holland, and eastern Germany. Eventually, these groups joined together and came to be known as the Anglo-Saxons. Within a hundred years of their arrival, they ruled most of the island.

The Anglo-Saxons worshiped many gods and goddesses, including Woden, who ruled over heaven; Thor, the god of war; and Freda, the goddess of peace. Pope Gregory I, leader of the Roman Catholic Church, taught the Anglo-Saxon kings about Catholicism beginning in 597. Eventually, most kings forced their people to convert, or adopt the new religion.

The Viking Era

Fierce warriors called Vikings, from Denmark and Norway, began invading in 789. They destroyed villages and murdered innocent people as they looked for gold, jewels, animals, and slaves to take home with them. By 865, Viking armies had conquered the north, east, and west. The south, then called the Kingdom of Wessex, was ruled by the Anglo-Saxon king Alfred the Great. Alfred the Great and his army resisted repeated Viking attacks in the 870s, including the Battle of Edington in 878. By the 1100s, the **descendants** of Alfred the Great had reclaimed large parts of the island.

King William I meets with English leaders to gain their support.

William of Normandy

Earl Harold became king in 1066, but his leadership was soon challenged by William of Normandy, who ruled a region of modern-day France. William of Normandy defeated Harold in the Battle of Hastings later that year. He took land away from Harold's people and gave it to his own followers. The new landowners became members of a class of **nobles**, who lived in lavish castles. Many people who had lost their lands to the nobles farmed the land and were called peasants.

Vikings came to England on ships called longboats that were decorated with colorful shields.

The Plantagenets were one of the mightiest families to rule England. Their reign began in 1154 with Henry II, who also ruled a large part of France. The famous warrior Richard the Lionheart was the second Plantagenet king. He fought bravely in the **crusades**.

Richard's son King John ruled between 1199 and 1216. People disliked King John because of the high taxes he imposed. Members of the nobility forced him to sign an agreement called the Magna Carta in 1215. The Magna Carta limited the king's rights to tax the people and restored some power to the noble class.

Difficult times

Problems did not end for the Plantagenets after John's reign. Beginning in 1337, England fought France in the Hundred Years' War, which cost the country money and lives. During this time, a disease called the Plague, or the Black Death, swept across Europe, killing nearly half of the English population.

War of the Roses

The Lancaster family took the throne in 1399, in the middle of the Hundred Years' War. Two years after the Hundred Years' War ended in 1453, a **civil war** broke out as the Lancasters and another family called the Yorks fought for control of England. The war was named the War of the Roses because the symbols of the families were the red rose of Lancaster and the white rose of York. Henry VII became the next Lancaster king when he defeated the Yorks during the bloody battle at Botsworth Fields in 1485.

A new church

Henry VIII, the son of Henry VII, took the throne when his father died. He was a cruel and greedy ruler, known for his spending habits and six wives, two of whom he **beheaded** and two of whom he divorced. The Roman Catholic Church did not allow divorce, so Henry VIII created a new Church with new rules. This new Church, called the Church of England, was Protestant, another denomination of Christianity. Henry VIII forced his subjects to convert, or adopt the new religion.

This portrait shows King Henry VIII, a member of the Lancaster family.

The Battle of Sluis, in 1340, took place during the Hundred Years' War.

In 1620, a group of pilgrims from England sailed to North America on a ship called the Mayflower. *Many were searching for a better life and religious freedom. The pilgrims founded the colony of Massachusetts in what became the United States.*

Back to Catholicism

Not everyone in England wanted to become Protestant, and violent rebellions erupted. After Henry VIII's son Edward took the throne in 1547, the **archbishop** Thomas Cranmer prepared a new book of prayer that he hoped would satisfy both Catholics and Protestants. The new prayer book followed the services of the Catholic Church, but, to please Protestants, it was written in English. Protestants believed that the Bible should be written in a language that everyone could understand, instead of the Latin language. When Mary I took the throne in 1553, she reestablished Catholicism as the main religion.

A prosperous time

England experienced a period of intellectual, political, economic, and artistic growth during the reign of Elizabeth I, between 1558 and 1603. This was the time of Sir Francis Bacon, who was a lawyer, **philosopher**, and author, and William Shakespeare, a poet and playwright. It was also a time of **exploration** and of conquering other lands. Ruthless pirates, such as Francis Drake, and explorers, such as Sir Walter Raleigh, sailed in search of riches and land.

After Elizabeth I

Queen Elizabeth I had no children, so when she died, King James VI of Scotland became King James I of England. During his reign, a group of Catholics who disagreed with his government tried to blow up the English **Parliament** Building. James I discovered the plot and executed, or put to death, the soldier sent to ignite the gunpowder, Guy Fawkes.

Islands under one rule

Since the early 900s, England's rulers have also controlled other parts of the island on which it is located. Wales, which was once a group of Celtic kingdoms, formally united with England after the Acts of Union were signed in 1536 and 1542. Scotland, Wales, and England all came under one rule when King James I took the throne in 1603. This led to the creation of Great Britain in 1707. Ireland, too, came under English control in the 1600s, but the union did not become official until 1800.

More reforms

By the reign of Charles I in 1625, members of the Parliament were angry because they felt the king had too much power. They wanted more input in running the country. A civil war broke out in 1642 between supporters of Charles I, called the Cavaliers, and supporters of the Parliament, called the Roundheads. The Roundheads were victorious in 1649 and ordered the execution of the king.

Oliver Cromwell

England became a commonwealth, or a country in which the central power is in the hands of the Parliament and the people, rather than the king or queen. The leader of the Roundheads, Oliver Cromwell, became Lord Protector, or ruler, of the Commonwealth and took power away from the king. Cromwell lowered taxes and worked to change the legal system, but he forced his strict **Puritan** beliefs on the people. He forbid pastimes such as card games, plays, and musical performances, and punished people who disagreed with him. The English soon lost faith in Cromwell and the commonwealth. When Cromwell died, the monarchy was restored and Charles II, son of Charles I, was on the throne.

The troubles in Ireland

Roman Catholics and Protestants continued to fight after the monarchy was restored. Charles II's son James II, who was a Catholic, ruled after him. Then, in 1688, Charles II's Protestant daughter, Mary, and her husband, the Dutch Prince William of Orange, removed James II from the throne. James fled to France and assembled a Roman Catholic army. He took the army to Ireland, where many people were unhappy with the Protestant government. In response, William and Mary sent a Protestant army to Ireland, which defeated James II's troops in 1690.

To prevent future attacks from Catholics, William sent a group of Protestants to live in the north of Ireland, now Northern Ireland. Disputes between Catholics and Protestants continue in Northern Ireland to this day.

Oliver Cromwell took power from the king after he defeated the king's army in the Battle of Naseby in 1645.

Modern England

In spite of years of religious and political struggles, England became the world's most powerful empire in the 1700s. After wars with the Spanish and French, England won land in the Caribbean, including the islands of Barbados and Jamaica. There, the English grew crops, such as tobacco and sugar cane, on **plantations** worked by slaves. The English brought the slaves, who were forced to work under terrible conditions, from areas they controlled in West Africa. Canada, India, and thirteen colonies in America were also under English control.

American independence

England's relationship with the colonists of America was peaceful until King George III, who ruled between 1760 and 1820, introduced heavy taxes on sugar, tea, and paper. The colonists did not want to pay taxes to a government in which they had no say. In 1773, some colonists protested by throwing 300 crates of tea into Boston Harbor in an event that came to be called the Boston Tea Party. This event led to the American Revolution, which lasted from 1775 to 1783. England lost its American colonies, but during this time it gained control of New Zealand and Australia.

During the Boston Tea Party, colonists dumped nearly 350 crates of tea into Boston Harbor.

Napoleon and the War of 1812

Tensions had existed for a long time between England and France because of struggles over land. The French general Napoleon Bonaparte, who was emperor of France between 1804 and 1815, tried to extend France's territory across Europe and a war broke out. During the war, England blocked French ships traveling to trade with other countries, including the United States. The United States responded by attacking Canada, which England controlled, in 1812. The War of 1812 ended two years later, when the United States and England signed a **peace treaty**. In 1815, England defeated Napoleon and gained control of France's territory in Africa.

The Industrial and Agricultural Revolutions

In the 1700s and 1800s, the Industrial and Agricultural Revolutions swept across England. They were called the Industrial and Agricultural Revolutions because new inventions revolutionized, or changed, farming and manufacturing, making them faster and easier. One of the most important inventions was the steam engine, which powered machines and trains. Farm workers moved to the city after new machines replaced them in the fields. They worked in newly opened factories, where they made little money for long hours in unsafe, dirty environments. Many people became ill or died in the factories and nearby mines.

Problems and change

In the 1820s, the government took steps to improve the lives of the English people. Trade unions, or organizations that fought for the rights of workers, became legal. The Factory Acts, which protected the rights of child and female workers, were passed in 1833, and slavery was abolished, or ended. Education and healthcare improved as the government built more schools and hospitals. New water and sewage systems were built, and gas heat and lighting became common. Many of these changes occurred during Queen Victoria's reign, from 1837 to 1901. This period became known as the Victorian Era.

World Wars

World War I was an international conflict that lasted from 1914 to 1918, in which Germany, Turkey, and Austria-Hungary battled England and its **allies**. Hundreds of thousands of English soldiers died in the brutal conflict. Peace was restored in 1918 and lasted until 1939 when Germany attacked Poland and started World War II. During this war, Germany bombed England during what was called "the Blitz." For more than eight months in 1940, Germany's air force dropped bombs on England's major cities and killed tens of thousands of people. Finally, in 1945, England and its allies defeated Germany.

(above) Steam engines, used in tractors and plows, revolutionized farming. This modern equipment made preparing fields for planting and even hauling heavy loads much easier.

(right) British soldiers move artillery in this photograph from the Boer War. The war between England and Dutch colonists called Boers was fought from 1899 to 1902 in what is now South Africa.

In this photo from 1946, British prime minister Sir Winston Churchill makes a "V," for victory, to celebrate the end of World War II.

Shrinking empire

The two world wars cost England a lot of money and the lives of millions. After World War II, food was scarce and goods were rationed, or distributed to people in small amounts. England's colonies in India, Africa, and the Caribbean declared their independence, following the example of countries such as Canada and Australia, which became independent in 1867 and 1901. Some former colonies joined the British Commonwealth of Nations, a group of countries allowed to rule themselves while keeping symbolic ties to England. Southern Ireland, unhappy with English rule, declared complete independence from England in 1922.

England today

England and its people still face many challenges. The government is trying to strengthen and promote new industries that declined during the World Wars, such as manufacturing electronics and pharmaceuticals, or medicines. England has also faced challenges with Scotland, Wales, and Northern Ireland, all wanting greater independence. These territories now have more control over their own affairs.

(above) From 1979 to 1990, Margaret Thatcher was England's first female prime minister. During her leadership, her government cut spending on health care, housing, and education, and fought a war in the Falkland Islands.

(below) The year 2012 marks the 60th anniversary of Queen Elizabeth II, the current Queen of England. The official Diamond Jubilee celebration, called Central Weekend, runs June 2-5, 2012, and will be marked by a national public holiday in England, Scotland, and Wales. Queen Elizabeth is the second longest serving monarch after Queen Victoria, who reigned for 63 years.

The people of England

England has many different regions, some of which began as small kingdoms ruled by invaders. Regardless of where they live, most English are descended from the Celts and Anglo-Saxons, although their customs, traditions, and **dialects** vary from place to place. For example, Cornwall, an area in the southwest, was settled by the Celts. Many people of Celtic ancestry still live there. They celebrate ancient Celtic festivals and some speak Cornish, a dialect of the Celtic language, Gaelic.

French immigrants

During the Hundred Years' War, many people who lived in parts of France ruled by the English escaped to England. French people also left their country in the 1700s because of civil wars. The island of Guernsey, in the English Channel, the body of water which separates England and France, became home to a large French-speaking community.

(top) A family in London reads about the royal wedding in a local newpaper.

(left) Friends have fun in the rain in England's Lake District.

16

Religious freedom

In the 1400s, Jewish **immigrants** arrived from France, Spain, and Portugal to escape religious **persecution**. Another wave of Jewish immigrants came from eastern Europe beginning in the 1930s, before World War II. In London, as well as in the western city of Liverpool and the eastern city of Cambridge, large Jewish communities worship freely at synagogues, which are Jewish houses of prayer.

New arrivals

Since the end of World War II, many immigrants have arrived in England from India, islands in the Caribbean, and other places that gained their independence from England. They came in search of jobs and because they were fearful of civil wars in their homelands after the English left. Today, large groups of people continue to arrive from parts of western Asia, India, China, and the Middle East. These people bring their religions, such as Hinduism, Buddhism, and Islam, with them. They also introduce new foods and languages to England.

In many towns and villages, local farmers sell their goods at open-air markets. Different regions are known for different products, such as sheep in the northwest and grains in the eastern part of England.

Approximately 90,000 people work in the office buildings at Canary Wharf, a major business district in London. This financial center features some of the tallest buildings in the country.

Country life, city life

Outside England's bustling cities, smaller towns and villages nestle among rolling green hills. Some small towns sprang up around stately homes where wealthy merchants and nobles lived. Others grew up around factories, such as the northern town of Bourneville, which was built around the Cadbury chocolate factory. Still other towns grew up around markets where farmers and craftspeople sold their wares. The streets where they set up their stalls were nicknamed "high streets." This is the name that many towns still give their shopping districts.

Small fishing boats dock in the Mousehole Harbor in Cornwall. Many people who live on England's coasts work as fishers and live in fishing villages.

Country homes

The most common type of home in the English countryside are thatched cottages. Their wooden frames are filled with a cement-like mixture made from materials such as earth, dung, straw, and stones. The roofs are made from thatch, which is tightly woven straw or reeds.

Most country homes are made from local materials. In parts of the north, such as the Pennine Mountains, people on farms live in longhouses built of a local stone called granite. The longhouses include living space for farm animals and a garage for farm equipment. In southeastern England, people live in weatherboard houses that were constructed in the 1700s and 1800s. Weatherboard houses were made with large boards that keep in the heat in the cool, rainy climate.

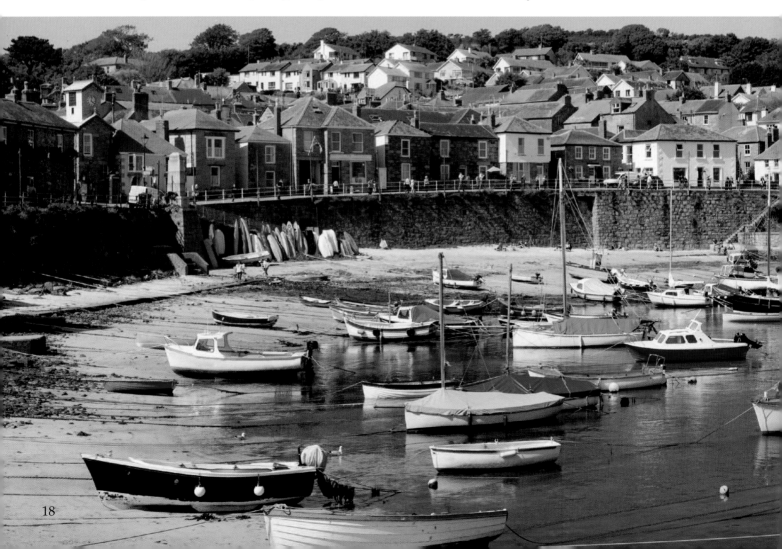

Life in the city

During the 1700s, many people moved to booming cities to find work. Cities grew so rapidly that there was a shortage of housing. Rows of attached homes, called rowhouses, were constructed so that as many people could live in as little space as possible. Today, London is the most densely populated part of England. About fifteen percent of the population lives there.

Cities declined after the Industrial Revolution and again after the world wars as manufacturing slowed down. Many cities that were dependent on industry fell into disrepair. In the late 1980s and 1990s, suburbs, or "New Towns," cropped up with new homes and office towers. The economy improved and more businesses moved into cities, often into old areas that had been restored. Tourism also brought new life to cities, with people from all over the world visiting England's museums, art galleries, theaters, and historic buildings.

(above) Ships bringing goods to and from England once docked at Canary Wharf, on the River Thames in London. Today, the area is home to office buildings, a shopping mall, a conference center, a railway and subway station, and parks.

Time to eat

What people in England eat depends on where they live. People on the east coast enjoy boiled or baked fish dishes such as Dover sole. In the southwest, people use sweet, juicy apples grown in local orchards to make cider and desserts called crumbles. Regions such as Stilton, in central England, are famous for cheeses used to make dips, soups, and salads.

Mealtime

Breakfast was once the largest meal of the day for farmers. It often consisted of bangers, which are sausages, served with bacon, eggs, and grilled mushrooms and tomatoes. People also ate lamb's kidneys, oatcakes, and "bubble and squeak," which is cabbage fried with potatoes. Today, most English people eat lighter meals for "brekkie," or breakfast. Dinner, served in the evening, is now the main meal of the day. Favorite dishes include steak and kidney pie, which is meat, vegetables, and gravy baked into a pie crust; shepherd's pie, which is ground beef or lamb covered in mashed potatoes; and battered sausages called toad-in-the-hole.

(above) Vendors from the countryside sell fresh fruits and vegetables, such as apples and brocolli, at an indoor market in Leicester.

(below) These friends have gathered at a cafe to indulge in a traditional full English breakfast.

Take away

In England, people call takeout food "take away." Some "take away" is served from stalls or vans called "chippers" that line busy city streets. People on their lunch breaks grab pasties, which are pastries filled with meat, vegetables, or fruit. People also order "take away," such as pizza, Chinese food, and spicy dishes of meat, fish, or vegetables called curries, to be delivered to their homes.

Puddings

Puddings can be a side dish, a main course, or a dessert. Yorkshire puddings are thick pastries made from flour, eggs, and animal fat, such as drippings from beef, that are baked and covered in gravy. These puddings are served with roast beef, potatoes, and vegetables. Bread and butter puddings are made by pouring custard, currants, and raisins over thick bread. They are served as side dishes or desserts. Spotted dick is a sweet dessert pudding made by steaming a mixture of flour, eggs, animal fat, and raisins. Once the cake-like pudding is done, it is covered in custard.

Other desserts

Fresh fruit, such as strawberries, apples, plums, and gooseberries, are used to make crumbles, tarts, and pies, or they are covered in fresh cream from local farms. Trifles are also popular desserts, with their layers of sponge cake, jam, fruit, custard, and whipped cream.

Chippers sell battered fish and chips, which are French fries, wrapped in newspaper to keep them piping hot.

Teatime

Many people in England have tea at four or five o'clock in the afternoon. This meal consists of small sandwiches filled with cucumbers or a spread such as fish paste; scones, which are a type of biscuit served with jam or cream; and pastries, such as cakes and cookies. These treats are served with a steaming pot of tea. The custom of having tea in the late afternoon began in the 1700s, when the **Duchess** of Bedford used to invite family and friends over for a snack. The afternoon snack was meant to keep them from getting hungry during a time when people ate only two meals a day. Today, "tea" means dinner, or the evening meal.

Family celebrations

In England, family and friends gather together to celebrate birthdays, weddings, and other special occasions. In Anglo-Saxon times, the English believed that being surrounded by family and friends kept evil spirits away from those celebrating birthdays. People also lit large bonfires to scare away the spirits.

In the Middle Ages, only kings and other wealthy nobles celebrated birthdays. They held large feasts, at which peasants living on their land brought them their best crops, meat, milk, or cloth as gifts. Today, everyone in England celebrates birthdays. A popular treat at children's birthdays is "the fortune cake." At one time, people added a coin and thimble to the cake mixture. It was believed that whoever received the piece of cake with the coin would be rich, and whoever received the thimble would never marry. Today, people bake coins or small toys into the fortune cakes.

(top) A boy blows out the candles on his birthday cake.

(bottom) A priest at St Bernard's Catholic Church in Lingfield, England, baptizes the baby of a Christian family. All the family members stand at the front of the church with the baby and watch the baptism.

Religious family celebrations

In Christian families, babies are baptized, or welcomed into the Church, by a minister or priest who pours holy water over the babies' heads. Around the age of seven or eight, some Christian children go to special classes to prepare for their first Communion. During Communion, Christians eat special wafers that symbolize the body of Jesus Christ and drink a sip of wine that symbolizes the blood of Christ. Confirmations take place when children turn thirteen. During the ceremony, children announce that they wish to become members of the Church. Family and friends come to church to witness these important events, and celebrate with a large meal afterward.

People from different countries have brought their own traditions to England. This Sikh bride and groom take part in a traditional wedding ceremony. Sikhism is a religion followed by many people in India.

Getting married

Many of today's wedding traditions began in England long ago. In Celtic times, when women were sometimes forced to marry, grooms and groups of strong men often captured brides. Anglo-Saxon grooms had friends, known as "bride's knights," bring their brides to the weddings. That way, grooms could be sure that their brides were not captured by other men who wanted to steal the brides' **dowries** or marry the women themselves. This evolved into the custom of grooms having attendants called best men.

People in England once thought it was good luck for female guests at a wedding to tear off a piece of the bride's wedding dress or part of the bouquet. Brides eventually began to toss their bouquet to the female guests, a custom that continues today. The tradition of eating wedding cakes with many tiers, or layers, began in Anglo-Saxon times. Wedding guests used to bring cakes instead of gifts and stack them on top of one another.

Family names

At one time, people in England had only first names. When the French, led by William of Normandy, took over England in 1066, they introduced French surnames, many of which changed over time. For example, the French surname "Beauchamps" became the English surname "Beecham." Other surnames, such as Weaver or Smith, came from people's professions, while surnames such as London, Ashby, or Baldock told where people lived.

 # A royal family wedding

People in England also celebrate the special occasions of the country's royal family. On April 29, 2011, Prince William, grandson of Queen Elizabeth II and second in line to the throne, married Catherine Middleton at Westminster Abbey in London. One million people lined the streets of London to catch a glimpse of the royal couple and to watch the service on two giant screens set up in Hyde Park and Trafalgar Square.

The service was watched by two billion people around the world on television and the Internet. This was the first royal wedding to embrace the Internet. A website and an "app" devoted to the wedding allowed the public a closeup view of the plans as the wedding day approached.

Royal titles

Upon their marriage, Prince William was given the title His Royal Highness The Duke of Cambridge and Catherine Middleton became Her Royal Highness The Duchess of Cambridge.

The day of the wedding was declared an official public holiday. Many people in England held neighborhood street parties in honor of the royal couple. A street party is a traditional celebration in which a neighborhood blocks off a street, sets up tables of food, and organizes games.

 # Sports and pastimes

Many sports were invented in England, including rugby and cricket. Over time, these sports spread to countries under British rule, and later gained popularity around the world.

(top) Girls play football, or soccer, at a school in Cirencester, England.

(bottom) Since 1877, the world's best tennis players have competed at Wimbledon, near London, in the only major tournament still played on grass, not turf.

Fabulous football

English football, known as soccer in North America, is played by people of all ages. Millions of fans watch professional football games on TV, or they attend matches dressed in their team's jerseys and colors to cheer on their favorite players. English football players, such as David Beckham, are celebrities, and many children hope to grow up and be professional football players themselves.

Rough rugby

Rugby is a rough game influenced by American football. Unlike American football, players do not wear a lot of protective equipment and many get injured during the games. To score a try, or touchdown, rugby players pass the ball to teammates beside or behind them, but not in front of them, until one touches the ball to the ground behind the goal posts. To score field goals, players kick the ball through the posts.

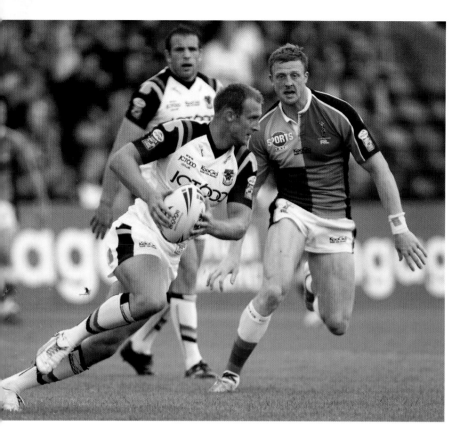

A player runs with the ball during a rugby game in London. Rugby balls are larger and rounder than those used in American football.

Come play cricket

Cricket is similar to baseball. A batter, called a striker, stands in front of a **wicket**. A pitcher, called a bowler, stands in front of another wicket. Beside him stands a runner, called a nonstriker, from the striker's team. The bowler rolls the ball along the ground and tries to knock over the wicket behind the striker. The striker tries to prevent this by hitting the ball with a bat. If the striker succeeds, the striker and nonstriker run between the wickets as many times as they can before a fielder, or player in the field, returns the ball to the bowler. Each time the striker and nonstriker switch places, their team scores a point.

A striker prepares to hit the ball during a cricket match between teams from India and England.

Gardening

The English enjoy gardening, whether it is in gardens surrounding their homes or on small plots, called allotments, that they rent in cities. Gardens surrounding thatched cottages are a mishmash of wildflowers that sometimes grow as high as the roofs on people's homes. More formal gardens have low hedges, usually made of lavender plants, that are carefully trimmed into rectangles, diamonds, circles, knots, and other shapes.

2012 London Olympics

The 30th modern summer Olympic Games will be hosted in London, England, in the summer of 2012, from July 27 to August 12. This is the third time the Olympic Games have been held in London, with previous Games taking place in 1908 and 1948. The City of London has transformed industrial land in East London into the Olympic Village that will host 10,500 athletes participating in 29 sports in 34 venues.

Many cities make sections of land called allotments available to city-dwellers to grow fruits and vegetables.

The Olympics goes green

London is the first summer Host City to plan for **sustainability**. Existing venues have been used where possible instead of all new construction. London's Olympic plan focuses on five areas that include minimizing greenhouse gas emissions and waste, encouraging a healthy and active lifestyle, and protecting the plants and animals in the area around the Olympic Village. After the Games, the Olympic Park will be transformed into one of the largest urban parks in Europe giving wildlife a home in the middle of the city. The Olympic Village will be converted into long-term homes for the local community.

(below) London Olympic Park
After the Games, the sports facilities and playing fields will be used by community sports clubs.

At school

Until 1880, many children in England did not attend school. Instead, they worked in fields and in factories. Most children who did receive an education were boys. They were taught by their parents, by private tutors, or they went to schools run by the Church or the town. Boys learned subjects such as mathematics, history, science, and philosophy. Mothers taught their daughters skills they needed to run a home, such as cooking, sewing, and weaving.

In the classroom

Today, both boys and girls go to school from the age of five to eighteen. They study subjects such as mathematics, science, history, English, and French. Younger students learn about England's history on day trips to castles and ancient ruins, while older children visit nearby countries on trips that last several days.

Boarding schools

England has many boarding schools, where children live and study. The first boarding schools were set up in the 1400s to prepare the children of wealthy families for a future as leaders and **scholars**. At schools such as Eton College, which was founded in 1440 by King Henry VI, children were taught politics and religion, in addition to other subjects. Nineteen of England's prime ministers and hundreds of its authors have studied there.

Many schools have uniforms that include a shirt, tie, and jacket for both boys and girls.

Important universities

For more than 700 years, students have studied in the classrooms and libraries of Oxford and Cambridge, two of the world's most respected universities. Both were founded by monks, or Christian holy men, and scholars who lived and studied together.

Oxford, in southcentral England, was founded in 1214. It is home to the Bodleian Library, the second largest library in Britain. Cambridge University was founded in 1284. It has a very famous museum, the Fitzwilliam Museum, with important collections of ancient Egyptian, Greek, and Roman **artifacts**.

Some students take their university classes over television, by mail, or on the Internet. This system, called the Open University System, began in 1970.

Accomplished students

Politicians, scholars, and religious leaders from around the world have studied at Oxford and Cambridge. Twenty-six of England's prime ministers, including Margaret Thatcher and Tony Blair, have attended Oxford. Former American president Bill Clinton also attended Oxford, as a Rhodes scholar. Rhodes scholars are outstanding students who are given full **scholarships** to study at Oxford for two or three years. Poet Alfred Tennyson and children's author A. A. Milne, who wrote Winnie the Pooh, attended Cambridge. Students from both universities have gone on to win Nobel Prizes, which are awarded to people who have shown excellence in areas such as mathematics, scientific discovery, and literature.

The University of Oxford has 38 colleges and six private halls.
Christ Church is one of the largest colleges that is part of Oxford.

29

William's trip to the park

"I'm all done with my chores!" William shouted as he burst through the front door of his house. William and his family live on a farm outside London. William's job is to help his father feed the cattle.

"Come get your brekkie then," his mother called to him.

William sat in front of a bowl of cereal and a cup of hot tea. "If I wait for the tea to cool down, I'll never get to school in time," he moaned.

"Add some milk and drink up," his mother replied. "You have a big day ahead of you." It was true. William and his class were going to South Hill Park, a national park near their school, to help repair a hedgerow.

(top) William, Rose, and some of their classmates look out the rear window of the school bus on their way to South Hill Park.

William's class had done many research projects on the importance of **hedgerows**. William and his friend Rose had learned that Anglo-Saxons once grew these fences, made from plants and trees, to protect their property from invasion. Over time, birds, rabbits, hares, and hedgehogs made their homes in the living fences.

"Do any of you have hedgerows on your land?" William's teacher asked the class. William raised his hand. His father and their neighbor, Mr. Yorke, had a long hedgerow between their properties that they worked very hard to maintain. William knew that many farmers cut down their hedgerows and replaced them with wooden or stone fences that were easier to take care of.

When they got to the park, William and Rose ran off the bus. Their tour guide, Simon, was waiting for them with small red sacks.

"Inside each sack is a seedling, or small tree," Simon explained. "There are hawthorn, blackthorn, hazel, maple, crab apple, and spindle seedlings." Rose whispered to William, "I didn't know there were so many types of trees in a hedgerow."

"You also have a trowel," Simon continued, "and a booklet about the animals and plants that live in the park. If you're quiet, you may see a rabbit or two."

Simon led the class to the hedgerow they were repairing. It was taller than most of the children in the class, including William. Simon showed the children how to dig a hole and plant their seedlings in places where the hedgerow's trees had died or animals and people had ruined them. When the children were done, they piled into the bus and headed home.

"Look!" William called to his parents as he burst through the front door. "Simon, our guide at the park, gave me a seedling for our hedgerow."

William's parents smiled. "How about we plant it after supper?" his father suggested. William couldn't wait.

(above) William walks along the hedgerow until he finds the perfect spot to plant his seedling.

(below) William's parents raise sheep on their farm. Low stone walls and hedgerows help keep the sheep from leaving their property.

Glossary

ally A country that officially supports another, especially during a war

altar A table or stand used for religious ceremonies

archaeologist A person who studies the past by looking at buildings and artifacts

archbishop A Christian religious leader who is responsible for an area called an archdiocese

artifact A product, usually historical, made by human craft

behead To chop off someone's head

civil war A war between different groups of people within a country

colony An area controlled by a distant country

conquer To overtake a country or people by force

crusade A holy war fought by Christians against Muslims to recover the Holy Land, the area where Jesus Christ lived and died

denomination An organized religious group within a faith

descendant A person who can trace his or her family roots to a certain family or group

dialect A version of a language

dowry The money or property that a bride brings to her marriage

duchess A wife or widow of a duke, who rules an area of land called a duchy

empire A group of countries or territories under one ruler or government

exploration The act of exploring, or traveling to new lands

hedgerow A row of bushes, shrubs, or trees that form a hedge

immigrant A person who settles in another country

Middle Ages The period in western European history from about 500 A.D. to 1500 A.D.

monarchy A government that is ruled by a king, queen, emperor, or empress

noble A person born into a high social class

pagan One who is not a Christian, Muslim, or Jew

Parliament The building where a country's law-making body meets

peace treaty An agreement signed by two or more warring countries to end hostility

persecution The act of harming another person for religious, racial, or political reasons

philosopher A person who studies or writes about the meaning of life

plantation A large farm on which crops such as cotton and sugar cane are grown

Puritan Belonging to a form of Protestantism from the 1600s and practicing simple forms of worship

Romans Belonging to an ancient empire that once covered territory from Egypt to England and ended around 410 A.D.

scholar A very knowledgeable person

scholarship Money given to a student to help pay for his or her education

sustainability The act of reusing materials in order to achieve or preserve an ecological balance

wicket A set of three sticks with two sticks resting on top, used in cricket

 # Index